Mary's Logic Puzzles Book 2

Mary Elder

Tellwell Talent
www.tellwell.ca

ISBN
978-0-2288-4322-1 (Paperback)

Table of Contents

#1
WEDDING ANNIVERSARY

The four O'Sullivan daughters were busy making arrangements for their parent's 40th wedding anniversary. Each daughter was responsible for two of the following duties, booking the hall, decorating, hiring a D.J., hiring the caterer, ordering the cake, preparing the speech, sending out invitations and selecting the wine. Knowing their parents would not slow down now that they are retired each daughter arranged for them to go on four very adventurous activities which include ice fishing, mountain climbing, white water rafting and a safari. From the following clues can you match each daughter with her two responsibilities for the big party and the surprise adventure she had booked as a gift for her parents.

1 Irene is in charge of decorations however she did not book the hall.

2 Sybil prepared the speech, she did not arrange mountain climbing.

3 The daughter in charge of the hiring the D.J. also selected the wine for the evening.

4 Wilma took care of the ice fishing trip to Alaska and Maxine handled the invitations.

5 The daughter in charge of the Safari trip also arranged the catering service.

6 No daughter's first name initial matches the first name initial of the adventure she was sending her parent's on.

	Task	Task	Adventure
Irene			
Maxine			
Sybil			
Wilma			

#2

BIRTHDAY BARBEQUE

Last night Jenny's husband with his three best friends and their wives arranged a surprise birthday barbeque for Jenny. The men took care of all preparations as well as the clean up to give the women a break. The meal included steaks, potato salad, tossed salad as well as Jenny's favorite desert Cherry Cheese cake. From the following clues can you match each wife with her husband and the dish each man made.

Note: Two of the men are Adam and Vince. The women are Anita, Jenny, Mavis and Vivian.

1 Marvin grilled the steak.

2 Anita's husband prepared the potato salad.

3 Jeff made the Cherry Cheese Cake.

4 Vivian's husband prepared the tossed salad.

5 No husband and wife share a first name initial.

	HUSBAND	DISH
Anita		
Jenny		
Mavis		
Vivian		

GREEK GODS

There is a small remote island in the Mediterranean Sea that is inhibited by great grand children of the Greek Gods. The men and women have a magical life compared to the rest of the world. Recently four men and their fiancées were wed in June on a different day 1st, 10th, 15th and 20th and each couple travelled to a different country for their honeymoon. From the following clues determine each man's new wife the day of their marriage and the country each travelled to on their honeymoon.

Note: One bride is named Aphrodite.

1 Apollo and his bride were married on a later date than Hestia and her husband but an early date than Dionysus and his bride.

2 Zeus and his wife enjoyed a wonderful time in a private chateau in France while Demeter and her husband relaxed in a country estate in England.

3 Hades and his new wife were wed on a later day in June than Hera and her husband but an early date in June than Demeter and her husband.

4 Hestia and her new husband were wed on the 10th of June and retreated to a glorious castle in Scotland.

5 Dionysus and his new wife spent their honeymoon at a private villa in Italy.

	BRIDE	DATE	COUNTRY
Apollo			
Dionysus			
Hades			
Zeus			

A DAY AT THE SPA

Jaunita and her three best friends love going to the spa once a month for some pampering. Last week the four women had two wonderful relaxing treatments each. From the following clues can you determine each woman's last name and the two special treatments enjoyed be each woman.

Note: One of the special treatments is a manicure.

1 Jaunita and Miss Vance had in some order the facial and the salt glow.

2 Noelle and Miss Landry enjoyed the pedicure and the deep body massage in some order.

3 Vivian loved the seaweed wrap and Miss Nickerson the aromatherapy session.

4 Miss Jones had a leg waxing treatment.

5 No woman has the same first and last name initial.

6 The woman who enjoyed the salt glow did not have the aromatherapy.

	Surname	Treatment	Treatment
Jaunita			
Lucille			
Noelle			
Vivian			

#5

DELECTABLE DISHES

My sister Evelyn is a terrific cook, she loves coming up with new recipes that fill the neighborhood with wonderful aromas. Each day last week Evelyn created a delicious meal using a special herb from her garden for each entrée, which simply makes each dish a dining experience. Six of her nearest neighbors could not resist the temptations and popped in on a different day throughout the week to ask Evelyn for the recipe she was working on. Evelyn agreed, however she said I am omitting the herb that gives each dish that special flavor which tingles the taste buds. One of the herbs Evelyn uses is thyme. The women all thanked Evelyn and hurried home to call their daughters to lend a hand in finding the missing herb to create the perfect dish as had Evelyn. Their husbands one of whom is Carl all thought this a terrific idea and suggested they invite Evelyn to dine with them and hopefully get her approval on each meal. The guys got busy searching for the perfect wine to compliment each dish and the women one of whom is Gail, with their daughters Anne, Joanne, Kim, Madison, Page and Reilly got busy experiment with different herbs. From the following clues can you match each woman with her daughter, husband, entree, wine and special Herb.

1 Gary's wife cooked a savory Leg of Lamb bursting with flavor.

2 Joanne's father selected a Chardonnay for his wife's entrée and Madison's dad picked a bottle of Beaujolais for their dining evening.

3 The missing herb Hal's wife needed was marjoram.

4 Dennis's wife prepared delicious Grilled Haddock and Carla made a mouthwatering Goulash.

5 The six daughters are Anne who helped her mom prepare a very succulent Prime Rib Roast, Thomas's daughter who found bay leafs to be her mom's missing herb, Marjorie's daughter, Kim whose dad selected a Cabernet wine, Jean's daughter and Reilly who helped her mom prepare a tantalizing seafood dish.

6 The Sauvignon complimented the Gumbo Shrimp very nicely, while the Cabernet was superb with the Lasagna dish.

7 Hugo's choice of wine was Chianti, while the Chardonnay enhanced the Grilled Haddock to perfection.

8 Page's dad selected a bottle of Bordeaux and her mom discovered rosemary to be her missing herb.

9 The six herbs each happy mom found to compliment her dish are bay leafs, Debbie's choice, basil which Jane discovered really brought out the flavor in her dish, oregano which went so well in a Lasagna dish, rosemary and Joanne's mothers.

10 No mother has the same first name initial as her daughter and no wife has the same first name initial as her husband.

11 Debbie prepared a scrumptious sea food dish while Kim's mom made mouth watering Lasagna.

Wife	Daughter	Husband	Entree	Wine	Herb
Carla					
Debbie					
Gail					
Jane					
Jean					
Marjorie					

#6
BROADWAY MUSICALS

Nigel and Cassie had just returned home from a fabulous and fun filled week in New York City. They had saved up especially for this trip, knowing they would have a life time filled with wonderful memories. Nigel booked the flight to arrive late Sunday night and depart early the following Sunday morning. A whole six days of visiting land marks, dining in famous restaurants and attending Broadway Musicals in the evenings, how exciting. Each restaurant they dined at was established in a different year, 1837, 1884, 1886, 1906, 1922 and 1926, some of these places are owned and operated by grandchildren of the original owners, how fascinating. At each musical Nigel and Cassie were thrilled to be introduced to a famous celebrity who had once starred in one of the shows although not the one attended at the time. From the following clues can you determine the day of the week from Monday to Saturday they visited each land mark, the restaurant they dined at, the year the restaurant was established, the musical they attended and the famous celebrity they met.

1 Nigel and Cassie were introduced to Olivia Newton John sometime earlier in the week than Catherine Zeta Jones but later in the week than Liza Minnelli.

2 The couple enjoyed a fabulous meal at 21 Club the same night they met Connie Wong at one of the musicals.

3 Nigel and Cassie were thrilled to meet Elaine Page after their day visit to the Empire State Building.

4 The happy couple dined at Delmonico's later in the week than their introduction to Meryl Streep, whom they met later in the week than dining at the restaurant established in 1926.

5 Nigel and Cassie attended the musical Cats sometime earlier in the week than Chorus Line but sometime later in the week than Chicago.

6 The Lion was established later than at least two other restaurants but earlier than The Palm. Nigel and Cassie dined at The Lion earlier in the week than Delmonico's but at least two days later than The Palm.

7 Nigel and Cassie attended the musical Mama Mia later in the week than Cabaret but earlier in the week than Chorus Line.

8 The happy couple had a wonderful time in Central Park later in the week than their visit to the Statue of Liberty.

9 Nigel and Cassie's six wonderful days in New York from Monday to Saturday in consecutive order are the visit to the National September 11th Memorial & Museum, the night they dined at the restaurant established in 1886, the night they attended the musical Cats, the night they met Elaine Paige, the day visit to the Metropolitan Museum of

Art and the night they dined at the restaurant established in 1837 before meeting Catherine Zeta Jones.

10 The six restaurants in order from oldest to newest established are the one they dined at after their day visit to Time Square, P.J. Clarke's where they dined later in the week than Keen's Steakhouse but earlier than 21 Club, the restaurant they dined at before attending the musical Grease where they met Meryl Streep, the one they dined at before meeting Olivia Newton John, the one they dined at after a day visit to Metropolitan Museum of Art and the Palm.

Week Day	Landmark	Restaurant	Year	Musical	Celebrity
Monday					
Tuesday					
Wednesday					
Thursday					
Friday					
Saturday					

#7

SCOTLAND

My husband Robert and I, him being of Scottish decent decided it was high time we made a trip to Scotland. Our daughter Maggie little to our knowledge was planning this for weeks because of our upcoming anniversary, her surprise gift to us. She had contacted seven of Robert's distant relatives and discovered each one lives near a castle including Achnacarry castle and a famous Loch one of which is named Lochy. Each male relative along with their wives, one of whom is named Olivia, thought this would be a wonderful opportunity to meet us and treat us to a tour of the Castles their Lochs and some delicious Scottish cuisine. Robert and I were so excited we could not wait to visit his home land, meet his distant relatives, and learn all about the castles their history and famous Clans one of which is MacDonnell who had once lived in each castle. From the following clues can you match each Castle with the near by Loch, the Clan who original owned the Castle, the male relative, his wife, and the delicious entree and dessert we enjoyed with each couple.

The seven castles in random order are as follows:

1 Tidram Castle, the one close to Loch Arkaig, the one previously owned by the Campbell Clan, the castle Kai and his wife took us on a tour, the castle where we dined with Brooke and her husband, the one we toured before dining on Roast Grouse and the one we toured before enjoying Berwick Cockles for dessert.

The seven Lochs in random order are as follows:

2 Loch Lomond, the Loch near Kilchurn Castle, the one associated with the Macfie Clan, the Loch near the castle were Oliver took us for a tour, the Loch near Emily's home, the when we hiked around before enjoying Chicken Tikka Masala and the Loch we hiked around before partaking in Apple Frushie for dessert.

The seven Clans in random order are as follows:

3 The seven Clans we were thrilled to hear about included the MacDonald Clan, the Clan who built Amhuinnsuidhe Castle, the Clan that Callum and his wife told us all about, the one Isla and her husband related to us, the Clan who once ruled the Castle where we dined on Boiled Gigot of Mutton, the Clan associated with Loch Awe and the Clan who had once owned the place where we enjoyed some delicious Marmalade Pudding.

The seven male hosts in random order are as follows:

4 Our seven wonderful hosts we spent our visits with are Lewis who lives near Loch Shiel, Aaron who lives near Boturich Castle, Jack who took us on a tour of the Castle that the Cameron Clan built, James with whom we ate Scotch Pie as an entree, the host whom we dined with on Roast Venison after our hike around Loch Quioch, Chloe's

husband and the host with whom we enjoyed delicious Caramel Shortbread with.

5 The names of some of the entrees we had were a little daunting but delicious none the same. The entrees we indulged in are Stovies which we had at Tidram castle, Haggis we enjoyed after our hike around Loch Lomond, the one we ate before our Blaeberry Pie while hearing of the Dunmore Clan, the meal we enjoyed with Skye and her husband, the entrée we had before hearing such wonderful I stories about the Cameron Clan, the one we enjoyed before having Dundee Cake and the one we enjoyed with Oliver and his wife.

6 Our seven gracious hostess's are Sophie, the one living near Loch Leosavay, Skye who lives near Dingwall Castle, Aaron's wife who regaled us we stories of the MacGregor Clan, Emily with whom we enjoyed Moffat Toffee for dessert with, Isla who lives near Glengarry Castle and James wife whom we enjoyed delicious Dundee Cake.

7 What a fascinating trip Robert and I had. The delicious desserts we enjoyed at each castle from Achnacarry to Tidram in order were Apple Frushie we had after our hike around Loch Arkaig, the Blaeberry Pie at Amhuinnsuidhe Castle, the Marmalade Pudding we enjoyed before hearing of the MacGregor Clan, the Berwick Cockles that Callum served us, the one we enjoyed with Isla and her husband which we had after dining on Roast Grouse, the one we had with James and the Moffat Toffee.

Castle	Loch	Clan	Husband	Wife	Entrée	Dessert
Achnacarry						
Amhuinnsuidhe						
Boturich						
Dingwall						
Glengarry						
Kilchurn						
Tidram						

8

COUNTY FAIR

Grandpa Roy's eight grandchildren are so excited, its county fair week. Grandstand entertainment, midway rides, craft exhibits, talent competitions and pie contests. The grandchildren each signed up to perform in a grandstand event one is pony racing. Their two aunts, two cousins, two uncles, and grandparents will be there to cheer the kids on and set up their own craft exhibits one of which is metal works. The grandchildren are also looking forward to enjoying the midway rides, one of which is the century wheel ride. The relatives will also be entering their special pies in a contest one of the pies is blueberry. To grandpa's great delight his grandchildren were also competing in the instrument playing talent show at night. What an exciting week this will be for all. From the following clues match each grandchild, six grandsons, Brennan, Connor, Dillon, Logan, Matthew, Riddick and two granddaughters Julia and Maddox with their grandstand event, their favorite midway ride, the craft exhibits they help each aunt, cousin, grandparent or uncle set up, the instrument they play at the evening competition and the type of pie each relative entered in the best pie ever contest.

1 The grandson who entered in the harness racing event helps one of his aunts set up her craft exhibit.

2 The grandson who gets a thrill out of the vertigo ride gives an uncle a hand with his woodworking exhibit.

3 Logan is entered in the harmonica playing competition and helps a cousin with his exhibit.

4 The granddaughter who loves to ride on the carousel plays the mandolin.

5 One grandson gives his grandfather a hand setting up his cane making exhibit.

6 The grandchild entered in the demolition derby event helps a cousin to bake key lime pie.

7 The eight grandchildren are in alphabetical order either from Brennan to Riddick or Riddick to Brennan are the one entered in the whip cracking event, the one who loves the orbiter ride, the one that assists granny with her quilt exhibit, the one entered in the chuck wagon race, the fiddle player who helps an aunt with her delicious caramel apple pies, the key board player, the one entered in the pickup truck pull event and the grand child who loves to go on the starship ride and helping an aunt with her pecan pies.

8 One cousin gets a hand setting up his glasswork exhibit from Matthew.

9 The grandson who rides the tilt a whirl plays the accordion.

10 The granddaughter who loves to help her aunt out at her jewelry exhibit took part in the corn hole digging event.

11 Dillon who entered in the saddle club riding show helps one of his uncles bake lemon meringue pies.

12 One grandson helps an aunt at her painting exhibit and plays the guitar, while Connor helps an uncle at his sculpture exhibit and with baking delicious chocolate whip cream pies.

13 One grandson plays the drums, while another grandson who rides the tilt a whirl enjoys baking cherry pies.

14 The grandson who rides on the enterprise helps bake pumpkin chiffon pies, while the grandchild who plays the banjo loves to go on the cliff hanger ride.

Grandchild	Grandstand Event	Ride	Craft Exhibit	Relative	Instrument	Pie
Brennan						
Connor						
Dillon						
Julia						
Logan						
Maddox						
Matthew						
Riddick						

9

DUET PART1: WONDERS of the ANCIENT & MODERN WORLDS

Three years ago the Branson's were on a quest to visit the seven wonders of the Ancient and Modern World, how to achieve this was the question. They contacted their closest friends whom they often traveled with to seek their thoughts. When the friends were all gathered together the ideas kept flowing like crazy, what a wonderful time exploring the many ways to travel be it by virtual reality or actual travel. Many of the Ancient wonders have been destroyed, however due to the Cave experience through virtual reality these wonders can still be much enjoyed by many whom chose to do so. Their friends of course where captivated by the quest and very much wanted to join in on the adventure. The first step was to book the Cave experience to see the Ancient Wonders of the World one is Pharos Lighthouse of Alexandria, and book flights for the seven wonders of the Modern world, one of which is Cabot Trail. From the following clues can you match each husband, Bill, Burt, Charles, Gene, Gerald, Jack and Ron, with his wife and their favorite Ancient and Modern Wonder of the World.

1 The Callaghan's were spellbound by the tranquility of the Pyramids of Egypt on the Ancient reality tour and Mount Everest one of the wonders of the Natural world.

2 Jack and his wife were enchanted by the Hanging Gardens of Babylon on their Ancient reality tour and Harbor at Rio de Janeiro on their Natural Wonder tour.

3 Betty and her husband rated the Temple of Artemis as their favorite Wonder of the Ancient World and the Colosseum of Rome as the best Medieval Wonder.

4 Elsie Melvin was enthralled with the Colossus of Rhodes as her Ancient Wonder and the Prehistoric Caves of France as her Natural Wonder of the World.

5 Ron and his wife were inspired by the majestic Mauseoleum at Halicanassus of the Ancient World and the Great Wall of China one of the Medieval World Wonders.

6 Grace Durant and her husband were touched by the Statue of Zeus on their Ancient tour and Hagia Sophia one of the medieval wonders of the world.

Husband	Wife	Ancient	Modern
Bill			
Burt			
Charles			
Gene			
Gerald			
Jack			
Ron			

#10
DUET PART2: WONDERS of the MEDIEVAL & NATURAL WORLDS

The Branson's and their friends were all rested up after the inspiring tours of the Ancient and Modern Wonders of the World, and are now ready for the next quest first to the Cave tour for the Virtual reality trip to the Medieval Wonders of the World one of which is Leaning Tower of Pisa, next travel to see the Natural Wonders of the World. From the following clues can you determine each couples shared surname, Medieval Wonder, and Natural Wonder each couple was dazzled by.

Note: One man has the same first and last name initial.

1 Gerald Jones and his wife were taking aback by the breathtaking view of the Great Barrier Reef in their Natural tour as well as Alaska Highway on their Modern travel.

2 Victoria Falls, one of the Natural Wonders of the World was described as dynamic by Bill Shirley.

3 Stella and her husband were captivated by Catacombs of Alexandria on the Medieval World tour and the Empire State Building Modern tour.

4 The peacefulness of the Grand Canyon was Dorothy's favorite Natural Wonder of the World.

5 Mary Evan's and her husband were touched by the timeliness of the Porcelain Tower of Nanjing on their Medieval reality tour and Taj Mahal on their Modern Wonder travel.

6 Paricutin Volcano in Mexico was Gene's favorite Natural Wonder of the World, while Joan and her husband chose Stonehenge as their favorite Medieval Wonder of the World.

7 Three Wonders of the Modern World are the Eiffel Tower that the Branson's thought the best, Golden Gate Bridge that Burt and his wife picked as number one and the Suez Canal chosen by the couple who had also picked Temple of Artemis at Ephesus as their favorite Ancient Wonder of the World.

Husband	Surname	Medieval	Natural
Bill			
Burt			
Charles			
Gene		26	
Gerald			
Jack			
Ron			

CLASSIC CARS

Ace and his five friends all love classic cars and each one owns a very special car they love driving and taking to car shows. Each guy is saving up to purchase a second classic car. The six cars each friend now owns are an Austin Martin, BMW, Ferrari, Lamborghini, Mercedes and a Porsche. The six cars they are saving for are a Corvette, Jaguar, Maserati, Mustang, Lincoln and Thunderbird. Their six girlfriends love the dedication and hard work their guys put into their cars as well as their relationships. The cars Ace and his friends own now were all made in a different year, 1935, 1953, 1965, 1978, 1990 and 1999. The cars of course are all in wonderful colors, Carlo Blue, Cinnamon Red, Cherry Red, Silver, Viridian Green and Bright Yellow. From the following clues can you match each man, with the car he owns, the year it was first made, the color, the car he is planning on buying and his girlfriend. Note the women are Amber, Brandi, Fern, Lacy, Megan and Pillar.

1 The Lamborghini was produced in a later year than Frank's car but an earlier year than Matt's car.

2 The Austin Martin which Fern loves driving around in with her guy was produced in a later year than the Porsche but an earlier year than the Carlo Blue BMW.

3 Lucy is so looking forward to driving in the Lincoln which will be beside the Mercedes in one man's garage.

4 Matt's new car will be beside a Cinnamon Red car in his garage.

5 Amber enjoys her rides in the bright Yellow colored car which was produced in a later year than the BMW but an earlier year than the Ferrari.

6 The six men are Brad, the man whose car was first produced in 1978, the man who will soon purchase the Mustang, Pillars boyfriend who will soon add a Thunderbird, Pete who purchased a Virdian Green and the man ready to purchase his dream Lincoln.

7 The six women are Fern whose boyfriend purchased the car first produced in 1965, Matt's girlfriend, Brandi whose boyfriend owns the silver car, Frank's girlfriend, Amber whose boyfriend is going to purchase a Jaguar and Lucy.

8 The cars in order of first production year to last are the one Lucy's boyfriend owns, the one soon to be partnered with the Porsche, the Austin Martin, Megan's boyfriends Maserati, Brad's car and the Ferrari.

9 Luke whose new car will be a Mustang which was produced in a later year than the Mercedes which is Cherry red but an earlier year than the Austin Martin.

Man	Car owned	Year Made	Color	Will Own	Girlfriend
Ace					
Brad					
Frank					
Luke					
Matt					
Pete					

DUET PART1: AUNT ROSIE'S CATS

My Aunt Rosie is a wonderful person, flamboyant, full of fun and very protective of her six cats and six dogs. Rosie acquired one canine and one feline at the same time and in the same way. One pair was left in a basket on her doorstep, three were gifts, one from a friend, a neighbor and an niece, one pair was purchased at the pet store and one pair were rescued from a shelter. Each cat and dog were the same age 2-7 when received at the same time. The six cats one of whom is Sheba all have wonderful personalities that the whole family find endearing. The cats also have a treat they enjoy the most. From the following clues can you determine the way Auntie Rosie acquired each cat, its breed one is a Tabby, personality, age and favorite treat.

1 Roxie the curious liver loving cat and the Welsh terrier were acquired in the same way they are neither the youngest nor the oldest pair.

2 The cat and dog received from Aunt Rosie's niece are the Manx and the dog who displays a very independent personality.

3 The playful Burmese was acquired at the same time as the charming Jack Russell.

4 Archie who loves his tuna was received at the same time as the Collie they are the youngest pair.

5 Caesar and the inquisitive cat who loves haddock were rescued from a shelter.

6 Hero and the dog with a stubborn personality were purchased from a Pet Store they are older than at least two other pairs and younger than at least two other pairs.

7 The Lhasa Apos enjoys her dog biscuits.

Acquired	Cat	Breed	Personality	Age	Food
Basket					
Friend					
Neighbor					
Niece					
Pet Store					
Shelter					

DUET PART2: AUNT ROSIE'S DOGS

Aunt Rosie loves her dogs as much as her cats. She recently held a birthday party for the pair who just turned five years old. Aunt Rose had plenty of food for all she thought it was a good idea to spoil her beloved animals on their special days. From the following clues can you match each dog in the manner he or she was acquired with the cat he shares a birthday with the breed of each dog one is an Irish Setter, personality, age and favorite treat one is jerky.

1 Sasha was the dog who just turned 5 years old along with the amusing Abyssinian who loves her chicken. Neither Sasha nor the Abyssinian cat where received as a gift.

2 Prince the clever dog was given to Aunt Rosie as a gift along with the very sociable Himalayan cat.

3 Alfie who loves milk bone was found in a basket on Aunt Rosie's door step he is the oldest dog and shares a birthday with the cat that enjoys salmon.

4 Jessie the Scottish terrier loves dental chews was received as a gift along with intelligent Mr. Jinx who loves bacon.

5 Shadow and the Russian Blue were gifts from a neighbor they will be celebrating their 4th birthday next month.

6 Tigger and the mischievous dog who loves rawhide treats are 3 years old.

7 The affectionate dog loves trail bits.

Acquired	Dog	Breed	Personality	Age	Treat
Basket					
Friend					
Neighbor					
Niece					
Pet Store					
Shelter					

＃14

THE BOTIQUE

Laura and her five friends are very gifted women. Each one has a passion for the items they create. The women all decided it would be a fabulous idea to purchase a boutique together to display their creations. Two of the women design a clothing line, one is lingerie and one is swim suits, one designs jewelry, the other three create bath oils, nail polishes and unique handbags. Having all agreed the boutique would be a great opportunity to display their goods they opted to launch the opening with a wine and cheese array to greet their customers. The six friends would each be in charge of one type of cheese Brie, Camembert, Gloucester, Gouda, Gruyere and Stilton as well as the wine that would complement their each choice of cheese and the perfect cracker, baquette or bread. Each woman also thought a mixture of fruit, olives or nuts would be a great idea. From the following clues can you match each woman with the item she designs, her selection of cheese, wine, crackers and her extra food item she contributed to the party.

Note: grapes are one of the extras. One wine is Pinot Blanc

1 The woman who makes fragment bath oils chose Camembert cheese and almonds, while another of the six chose olives with grain crackers.

2 Estelle who designs either the swim suits or the lingerie selected a fruit to accompany her cheese choice.

3 The woman who designs fabulous hand bags chose Gloucester cheese and Melba toast.

4 Kate selected a Merlot to accompany her cheese while another woman chose a Riesling to enhance the Stilton cheese.

5 The nail polisher creator selected Gruyere cheese and cashews, while the woman who selected Brie cheese also opted for French bread.

6 The woman who designs jewelry selected Gouda cheese, while Paula who does design one of the clothing lines chose crispy crackers and pecans.

7 Laura who does not design jewelry included dates in her shopping trip.

8 Allison selected Champagne and baquette loaf while Michelle added Gruyere to enhance the Sauvignon Blanc and water crackers.

9 The swim suit designer chose a Chardonnay wine.

Woman	Creation	Cheese	Wine	Cracker	Side
Allison					
Estelle					
Kate					
Laura					
Michelle					
Paula					

#15
NATURE WALKS

Eleanor loves the great doors one of her favorite activities is walking the nature trails near her home town. Last week Eleanor her husband and four of their friends spent the day hiking the trails near their home town. While on their walk they came across three chipmunks and three squirrels. Each rodent was snacking on a different type of food which included acorns, berries, leaves, mushrooms, roots and worms, near a brook, creek, pond, river, stream or waterfall. Each of the friends could not resist giving the adorable rodents a name one of which is Theodore. Each spotted a different type of bird as well. From the following clues can you determine the chipmunk or squirrel each person spotted, the name they chose, the food, one is worms, each was nibbling on, body of water and the bird.

Note: Two of the birds spotted are a Horned Owl and a Lorikeet.

1 Eleanor's husband could not resist naming the chipmunk he spotted Alvin.

2 The squirrel named Cheeks by one of the women was gnawing on leaves.

3 One of the men was the first to spot a squirrel near a brook and the Macaw in a tree.

4 The woman who first saw the Blue Jay named her squirrel Sheldon.

5 The Osprey was first seen by one of the men whose rodent was munching on his treat near a creek.

6 Shawna spotted one of the two owls seen that day after she noticed a chipmunk near a waterfall.

7 The chipmunk Brian spotted first was nibbling on berries.

8 The snowy owl was spotted after a squirrel was seen near a river

9 One rodent was eating acorns near a stream.

10 The squirrel gnawing on roots was spotted by one of the men.

11 The three men are Gary whose chipmunk was eating mushrooms, the one who named his squirrel Flash and the one who called his chipmunk Simon who was near a pond.

12 Eleanor did not see the snowy owl first.

Person	Type of rodent	Name	Food	Water	Bird
Brian					
Charlene					
Eleanor					
Gary					
Jason					
Shawna					

#16

FLOWER GARDENS

Marilyn loves flowers and her husband loves to garden, how wonderful is that. This year Marilyn's husband planted three new varieties of flowers one of Roses one of Irises and one of Marigolds in three different colors. Seven of their neighbors were very impressed and decided to follow suit. From the following clues can you determine each husband his wife, the type of Roses, Irises and Marigolds each planted and the color each chose.

NOTE: One woman's name is Marion: One variety of Irises is Loyalists and one color is Magneta.

1 The three white flowers are the Belgian Princess Irises which Marilyn's husband planted, the First Kiss Marigolds which George planted and the Moon Dance Roses planted by Sally's husband.

2 The flowers planted in red are the Titan's Glory Irises planted by Kevin, the Fatima Marigolds planted by Irene's husband and the Radiance Roses planted by Zoe's husband.

3 The three purple varieties are the Moon Song Marigolds, the Bombay Sapphire Irises planted by Ethan and the Prairie Rose Roses.

4 The three primrose colored flowers are the English Charm
Irises planted by Rose's husband, the Bride to be Marigolds
planted by Keith and the American Beauty Roses planted
by Bill.

5 The three gold colored flowers are the Instant Smile Irises
planted by Yvonne's husband, the Cameo Marigolds
which were in the same garden as the Moon Dance
Roses and the Diane Grace Roses planted by Dan.

6 Larry's wife was very pleased with the lavender shade of
the Blue Flirt Irises he grew for her, while Rose loved the
lavender Blended Beauty Marigolds and Sean's wife was
very happy with her lavender Heritage Roses.

7 Louise loved her orange colored Moon Journey Irises and
her Blended Blush magenta colored Roses, while Yvonne
loved her orange colored Lady Mix Marigolds and Keith's
wife loved her orange colored Gold Blush Roses.

8 Irene loves the Prairie Rose purple colored Roses her
husband planted, Marilyn loves her American Beauty
Roses and Zoe loves her Dark Magic Marigolds.

Husband	Wife	Irises	Color	Marigolds	Color	Roses	Color
Bill							
Dan							
Ethan							
George							
Keith							
Kevin							
Larry							
Sean							

Solutions

#1

Irene	Decorations	Cake	Mt. Climbing
Maxine	Invitations	Catering	Safari
Sybil	Speech	Hall	Water Rafting
Wilma	D.J.	Wine	Ice Fishing

#2

Anita	Vince	Potato Salad
Jenny	Marvin	Steaks
Mavis	Jeff	Cherry Cheese Cake
Vivian	Adam	Tossed Salad

#3

Apollo	Demeter	15th	England
Dionysus	Aphrodite	20th	Italy
Hades	Hestia	10th	Scotland
Zeus	Hera	1st	France

#4

Jaunita	Nickerson	Facial	Aromatherapy
Lucille	Vance	Manicure	Salt Glow
Noelle	Jones	Pedicure	Leg Wax
Vivian	Landry	Sea Weed Wrap	Massage

#5

Carla	Madison	Thomas	Goulash	Beaujolais	Bay Leaf
Debbie	Reilly	Hal	Gumbo Shrimp	Sauvignon	Marjoram
Gail	Kim	Carl	Lasagna	Cabernet	Oregano
Jane	Anne	Hugo	Prime Rib	Chianti	Basil
Jean	Page	Gary	Leg of Lamb	Bordeaux	Rosemary
Marjorie	Joanne	Dennis	Gr. Haddock	Chardonnay	Thyme

#6

Monday	Nat. Sept 11th Memorial	Palm	1926	Chicago	Liza Minnelli
Tuesday	St. of Liberty	Keen's Steakhouse	1886	Grease	Meryl Streep
Wednesday	Central Park	The Lion	1906	Cats	Olivia Newton John
Thursday	Empire State Building	P.J. Clarke	1884	Cabaret	Elaine Paige
Friday	Metropolitan Museum of Art	21 Club	1922	Mama Mia	Connie Wong
Saturday	Times Square	Delmonico's	1837	Chorus Line	Catherine Zeta Jones

#7

Castle	Loch	Clan	Husband	Wife	Entrée	Dessert
Achnacarry	Arkaig	Cameron	Jack	Sophie	Boiled gigot of mutton	Apple Frushie
Amhuinnsuidhe	Leosavay	Dunmore	Kai	Chloe	Chicken Tikka Masala	Blaeberry Pie
Boturich	Lomond	MacGregor	Aaron	Brooke	Haggis	Marmalade Pudding
Dingwall	Quoich	MacFie	Callum	Skye	Roast Venison	Berwick Cockles
Glengarry	Lochy	MacDonnell	Oliver	Isla	Roast Grouse	Caramel Shortbread
Kilchurn	Awe	Campbell	James	Olivia	Scotch Pie	Dundee Cake
Tidram	Shiel	MacDonald	Lewis	Emily	Stovies	Moffat Toffee

43

Brennan	Harness Racing	Star Ship	Painting	Aunt	Guitar	Pecan
Connor	Pickup Truck Pull	Cliff Hanger	Sculptures	Uncle	Banjo	Chocolate Whip Cream
Dillon	Saddle Club Riding	Vertigo	Wood Working	Uncle	Key Board	Lemon Meringue
Julia	Corn Hole Digging	Century Wheel	Jewelry	Aunt	Fiddle	Carmel Apple
Logan	Chuck Wagon Race	Enterprise	Metal Works	Cousin	Harmonica	Pumpkin Chiffon
Maddox	Pony race	Carousel	Quilts	Granny	Mandolin	Blue Berry
Matthew	Demolition Derby	Orbiter	Glass Blowing	Cousin	Drums	Key Lime
Riddick	Whip Crack	Tilt a Whirl	Canes	Grandpa	Accordion	Cherry

#9

Bill	Betty	Temple of Artemis at Ephesus	Suez Canal
Burt	Elsie	Colossus of Rhodes	Golden Gate Bridge
Charles	Stella	Pyramids of Egypt	Empire State Building
Gene	Grace	Statue of Zeus at Olympia	Cabot Trail
Gerald	Joan	Pharos Lighthouse of Alexandria	Alaska Highway
Jack	Mary	Hanging Gardens of Babylon	Taj Mahal
Ron	Dorothy	Mauseleum at Halicanassus	Eiffel Tower

Bill	Shirley	Colosseum of Rome	Victoria Falls
Burt	Melvin	Leaning Tower of Pisa	Prehistoric Caves of France
Charles	Callaghan	Catacombs of Alexandria	Mount Everest
Gene	Durant	Hagia Sophia	Paricutin Volcano of Mexico
Gerald	Jones	Stonehenge	Great Barrier Reef
Jack	Evans	Porcelain Tower of Nanking	Harbor at Rio de Janeiro
Ron	Branson	Great Wall of China	Grand Canyon

Ace	Mercedes	1935	Cherry Red	Lincoln	Lucy
Brad	Lamborghini	1990	Bright Yellow	Jaguar	Amber
Frank	BMW	1978	Carlo Blue	Maserati	Megan
Luke	Porsche	1953	Silver	Mustang	Brandi
Matt	Ferrari	1999	Cinnamon Red	Thunderbird	Pillar
Pete	Austin Martin	1965	Viridian Green	Corvette	Fern

Basket	Sheba	Burmese	Playful	7	Salmon
Friend	Archie	Himalayan	Sociable	2	Tuna
Neighbor	Roxie	Russian Blue	Curious	4	Liver
Niece	Mr. Jinx	Manx	Intelligent	6	Bacon
Pet Store	Hero	Abyssinian	Amusing	5	Chicken
Shelter	Tigger	Tabby	Inquisitive	3	Haddock

#13

Basket	Alfie	Jack Russell	Charming	7	Milk Bone
Friend	Prince	Collie	Clever	2	Jerky
Neighbor	Shadow	Welsh Terrier	Affectionate	4	Trail Bits
Niece	Jessie	Scottie	Independent	6	Dental Chews
Pet Store	Sasha	Lhasa Apso	Stubborn	5	Dog Biscuits
Shelter	Caesar	Irish Setter	Mischievous	3	Rawhide

#14

Allison	Bath Oils	Camembert	Champagne	Baquette	Almonds
Estelle	Swim Suits	Brie	Chardonnay	French Bread	Grapes
Kate	Jewelry	Gouda	Merlot	Grain Crackers	Olives
Laura	Hand Bags	Gloucester	Pinot Blanc	Melba Toast	Dates
Michelle	Nail Polish	Gruyere	Sauvignon	Water Crackers	Cashews
Paula	Lingerie	Stilton	Riesling	Crispy Crackers	Pecans

#15

Brian	Chipmunk	Simon	Berries	Pond	Lorikeet
Charlene	Squirrel	Cheeks	Leaves	River	Snowy Owl
Eleanor	Squirrel	Sheldon	Acorns	Stream	Blue Jay
Gary	Chipmunk	Alvin	Mushrooms	Creek	Osprey
Jason	Squirrel	Flash	Roots	Brook	Macaw
Shawna	Chipmunk	Theodore	Worms	Waterfall	Horned Owl

Bill	Marilyn	Belgian Princess	White	Moon Song	Purple	American Beauty	Primrose
Dan	Rose	English Charm	Primrose	Blended Beauty	Lavender	Diane Grace	Gold
Ethan	Zoe	Bombay Sapphire	Purple	Dark Magic	Magenta	Radiance	Red
George	Louise	Moon Journey	Orange	First Kiss	White	Blended Blush	Magenta
Keith	Marion	Loyalists	Magenta	Bride To BE	Primrose	Gold Blush	Orange
Kevin	Sally	Titans Glory	Red	Cameo	Gold	Moon Dance	White
Larry	Irene	Blue Flirt	Lavender	Fatima	Red	Prairie Rose	Purple
Sean	Yvonne	Instant Smiles	Gold	Lady Mix	Orange	Heritage	Lavender